MW00779679

73

Said the Manic to the Muse
a collection of poetry

ℭℬ

by Jeanann Verlee

Write Bloody Publishing
America's Independent Press

Austin, TX

WRITEBLOODY.COM

Verlee, Jeanann.
1ˢᵗ edition.
ISBN: 978-1-938912-96-2

Cover Designed by Ashley Siebels
Author Photo by A. Pavhk
Proofread by Sarah Kay and Alex Kryger
Edited by Jon Sands, Adam Falkner, Angel Nafis, Ian Khadan
Interior Layout by Andie Flores
Type set in Bergamo from www.theleagueofmoveabletype.com

Printed in Tennessee, USA

Write Bloody Publishing
Austin, TX
Support Independent Presses
writebloody.com

To contact the author, send an email to writebloody@gmail.com

MADE IN THE USA

Said the Manic to the Muse

Jeanann Verlee

Said the Manic to the Muse

I

II

III

I

Force not the parent's hand to slay the child.

—Medea, Euripides

THE SESSION

Say alone. *Forty times. Pair it with the desert.* Say it.
Alone. Alone. Alone. Say the words plain, she says.

Say it plain. Say it outright. *Alone.* Don't get poetic.
Say I. Say me. Say I am alone. Say your age, she says.

Thirty-six, I say. Say it, she says. *I am thirty-six.*
Own it. *I am alone. I am thirty-six.* She says tell me

about the children. Don't use metaphor. I say, *Blue eyes.*
It's only a guess. We have—not we, she corrects—*I*

have blue eyes. It's only a guess. Tell me about the children.
There are hundreds, I say. Punch myself in the stomach.

Hundreds. She says no, tell me about your children.
Tell you about the dead? No, she says, no one died.

Say it clear, stop the poetry. I say, *The children in our*—
no, my—*future are hard marbles sunk to the bottom*

of a fish tank. No. There is no fish tank. There are no
marbles. She is growing irritable. I say, *There are no*

children. There. I stop talking. She asks more questions.
I am mute. I am thinking of my sheets. Thinking of my

molding bathtub and how much blood could fill it. I think
of a poem written by a friend about a tubful of teeth.

I think about teeth falling out of my face. About my face
opened by a bullet's exit. She asks what I am thinking about.

I say, *Peanut butter.* What about peanut butter? I say, *I'm*
lying. She says why? I say, *There are no children. Never.*

I punch myself in the stomach. She says stop or I will
restrain you. I dig my nails into the armrest. Don't

damage the furniture, she says. I say, *Peanut butter.*
She says the session is over.   There is no she.

It's just a subway car and a Tuesday morning
where the fluorescent lights are flickering so loud,

it almost drowns out the voices telling me that
I will die today. No one ever believes this story.

CHILDREN MADE OF COTTON

My son asks where he came from.
It is my first lie. I say, *I brought you home*
from a place where hundreds of little lamb-boys live.
He says, *Really!?* I say, *Yes, and I almost*
couldn't choose. Then you, so bright and soft.
I put you in my cart and went straight to the checkout line.
He furrows his plush brow, *Hrmph!*
I ask him what's wrong. He says, *If it was so easy,*
why didn't you bring my brothers?
I tell him he has plenty of brothers,
pointing to the others strewn across the bed.
No, Mama, he whispers, *it isn't the same.*
He tucks his head down, covers his eyes with his ears.
I'm completely without answers.
My second lie is to tell him the laundry is perfectly safe.
I watch him bob at the water's soapy rim, gurgling and straining,
fighting the impossible pull. He wails on his way to the dryer.
When I retrieve him I find grid marks burned into his rump.
He says he forgives me and I begin to cry. A raw,
convulsive kind of sob. I go like this for hours.
The third lie he never believes.
I tell him, *Mama loves all her children just the same.*
When he asks if I have real children I tell him,
You are real, and you are mine. He pouts.
Says, *Mama, stop it. I know I'm only made of cotton.*
All of my bones break at once.

As Your Body Becomes an Invitation

Your breasts are firm as wood. Swollen, milkthick.
Carry in them a stern ache. At daybreak,
the familiar rip in your abdomen.
There was a time you didn't know your body this well.
Thirteen. Twenty-five. But you are thirty-six and your hips
have rotated outward: a slow earthquake.
Thighs, once thin as baseball bats, shifted down,
a thick braid of extra muscle.
Your feet have widened, remarkable and strong.
You, in the mirror, are a different animal. Your trunk
is a readied ship, shaped a perfect hourglass.
Your lips, all of them, plump.
Your femurs part like wishbone.
Spine, welded to pelvis. You are sturdy. Unbreakable.
It is dawn and your body moans its expected elegy.
But today, your organs flinch. It comes. An open spigot.
Your body is a drain. An evacuation.
The opened aorta that spills. And spills.
This is a new undoing. You. Standing wide
over bathroom tiles. Your good legs, a red massacre.
There is not enough cotton to pack this wound.
You mop the tide with the nice towels your mother sent.
The blood rises, drowns the marbles of your toes,
steeps your anklebones in a thick aroma of meat.
Such easy murder.
You press your stained hands to your breasts.
How long since anyone has taken them in their mouth?

FLEEING THE MURDER (THE CHILD)
after an artist's rendering of the author's mother, titled "Medea"

I must also admit, the portrait hurt. Curdled the beast inside me.
  The artist's cruel divination. His hollowing, and the mutilation of skin.
Naming you *Medea*.   How the mother in me hurled from my throat.
    A gasp. Clench. Rage. Compelled to protect you.
        (The child becomes the mother.)
  To cradle your morphed bones, reconstruct your harrowing beauty.
Return to you everything I stole.   (The child ruins the mother.)
  How desperate I became.   To erase. To unmake my mouth, my pulse.
To unlive.   Return all you sacrificed.   Offer a small chance at joy.

GENETICS OF REGRET

I'm sorry I don't call. Sorry I snuck down the stairs & out
to the mouth of a boy who will never know my name.
I'm sorry I ruined your carpet with a backdraft of whiskey.
Sorry I told our secrets. Put them in a book. Didn't tell you about it.
I'm sorry for the freckles & the switches
& the mean boys in grade school.
I'm sorry I scratched your Neil Diamond record.
Drew the picture of the dead cat. Titled it after my dead sister.
I'm sorry they pulled her from your body like a sad wet sponge.
I'm sorry no one came to the hospital. Sorry I felt sorry.
I'm sorry about the stolen tampons & the nest of mice in the stove.
The pennies for gas money. Sorry I drank all your rum.
For the boy in the basement. & the one on the porch.
& the back of your car. The slashed window screens. & forearms.
Sorry I lied about acid & the boy with the knife.
The houseful of beer rats. Sorry for the weevils & the dead grass.
I'm sorry I don't call anymore.
I'm sorry your life looks like this in photo albums.
That I was part of your stain. That it took 36 years to say this.
You hate me. You are too kind to say so.
I'm sorry I told our stories. I am low. I never thanked you
for sacrifice. For stereo & dolls & English & correcting my stutter
& the big slumber party with all the gift bags.
Sorry I vomited in the wash drain. Sorry I left. Sorry I came back.
You still get ferocious. Sorry I struck back. Loved you *so hard*—
then turned like a coin that has run out of spin.
I'm sorry the rock opened that boy's forehead. That I cursed you.
Wouldn't let you hit me anymore. I'm sorry I lied. I am a coward.
My skin has started to yellow. My neck is curving
into an ampersand. We can't talk about it. We can't talk.
Sorry the world kicked you this hard. Sorry he's sick, Mama,
& all I can do is worry what happens next.
I wrote the poems. I stopped calling. I don't visit. I'm sorry
you never wanted me. Sorry I don't need you like other girls.
There's too much decay. No grandchildren. I failed.
I am alone. Alone is easier than talking to you.

I'm sorry it comes like this, flood & undertow.
Can't sit comfortably in the same room, I twitch like a startled moth.
Sorry I came out hard & sharp & full of claws. Ruined your body.
Only learned the wrong things.
I'm sorry I don't call. I'm sorry you are too far.
Sorry I have no intention of coming to find you.

MATHEMATICIAN

She counts backward most days.
Starts always at today, inches toward birth.

Men want little to do with numbers.
Instead: barbecues, hammers, art. The growl of heavy machinery.

Women count.

Coins in jars, days to paycheck, each nephew's baby teeth.
Count, like abacus: three daughters, five forks, eighteen weeks.
This, the days until Thanksgiving.
This, the number of snapdragons laid at Grampy's grave.
This, the ounces of blood lost to children unhatched.

She paces the city, muttering numbers.
Passersby hear her ticking, watch her metronome hips.
Her body is a sturdy clock.
A miracle of arithmetic.

Her belly, a basket of tallied eggs.

After the Bridal Shower

His name is a clock you hang above the stove.
You cook better than his ex. His mother.
Babies reach for your breasts from passing strollers.
Kittens yowl down from windowsills for milk.
Men swarm your waist like hungry bees.
Dogs chase you for praise.
Your hips are an invitation. Your face, a love letter.
He is sitting beside you. Silent.
You wait. Like a lady.

THE PROPOSAL

Strangers gawk in awkward amazement.
Her once unspoiled skin, cracked and peeling.
The smell of char as she passes.

A constant, almost inaudible sizzling.
Heat pours off her shoulders like a bad radiator.
She moves between tables, sipping other people's

bourbon, laughing at unintentional jokes.
Wears a collar of orange flames, little else.
Friends offer up water glasses, chase after her

with wintry coats, patting down the flare.
She offers charmed giggles, politely
removes patches of skin as they curl upward.

Plucks fried hair in wiry clumps, peels away
shriveled chips of blackened muscle.
In passing whispers, friends recount the tale:

her lover arrived at her door,
knelt at her feet, reached to his pocket.
How tears swelled out and down her face,

lips already mouthing the word *yes*.
Then, in his hands, only matchsticks and butane.
How he doused her toes. How loud the rumble.

DAYDREAM

Today, at 6:38 PM, a bundle of
pink balloons rose skyward
outside my 14th floor window
somewhere along 54th Street.
I thought for a moment it was
you, finally arrived. A dramatic
entrance. Tuxedoed, landing on
the ledge, pressing a smile into
the glass. Instead, a long fray of
red ribbon. Not even a wrist,
not a single finger.

WE'RE HAVING A BIRTHDAY PARTY

I twisted crepe paper across the walls in the girls' room.
Strung balloons in a row up the banister.
Stuffed polka-dotted gift bags with candy necklaces,
Ring Pops, neon glow bracelets.

Added blow bubbles, baseball cards, and figurines
of both Piglet and Winnie-the-Pooh. I made fruit punch,
and bought soy milk (for Harold's sensitive tummy).

Baked peanut butter cookies (your favorite)
by Mallory's request, and chocolate cake—Kimberly helped
with the icing! Suzie wanted popcorn and little Connor
asked for Cheetos. A bowlful of gummy worms

for the twins (they eat just like their Dad).
We'll play Twister and charades, and Chinese checkers—
except for Samantha and Jared who want to play chess.

Later, I'll put on your mother's Motown records
for dancing. Caroline's wearing her tap shoes,
Isobel's in a tutu, and Marcus worked out a whole routine
to *Papa Was a Rollin' Stone*.

Don't be startled, dear. Our children were born this morning:
extracted with tweezers, one by one. Left the bathroom
a bit of a mess. Blood all over the shower curtain,

ovaries clogging the drain. Fallopian tubes falling out,
I used your brother's welding rod to cauterize.
Accidentally melted the jars of cream by the sink, the paint
off the back of the door. Ignited a bottle of Drano.

Still, I think the party will be a delight. The children are giddy
Unfortunately, darling, everyone agreed: you are not invited.

GRIEF, NOT GUILT

I wish you a tongue scalded by tea.
A hangover. Burnt toast. Stubbed toes. A lost job.
I wish you weeping in the shower. Salt in the sugar bowl.
A wish list of sorrows. Grief, not guilt.
Hole in your favorite coat. Stain on the good suit.
Arthritis for your joints. A broken guitar string at every show.
I wish each breath a little harder. Each workday
an hour longer. I wish your heart a thousand breaks.
All your sports teams, bottom rank. I wish your friends
go quiet. The leaves brown above your head.
A thunderstorm every morning. Nothing but pearls
when you shop for her diamond. I wish you bad knees,
a sore back. Empty sheets. A ghost to haunt your house.
A tub brimming with mud. Closet stuffed with too-small shoes.
Flat beer. Sour milk. Weak coffee. I wish you flat tires,
soggy pasta, a tax audit to fail. Bent forks, dull knives.
A hangnail for every finger.
I wish you a chamber filled with empty bassinets.
A room wallpapered with my photographs.

A Boy Named Never

My chest is a birdcage
where two canaries are perched,
chirping and preening their feathers.

Today, a little boy came to my door.
I thought he was selling chocolate bars for class,
but he didn't say a word, just pressed his tiny hand
through my sternum, precise as a surgeon.

He pulled out one of the canaries.
Walked away humming a lullaby,
kissing her soft yellow head.

UNWRITING YOU

Your stitches
loosen and your face
unravels and your
lips fall to the tiles
and your tongue
dries to dust and your
fingers unhinge and
your chest sinks
and your mother
forgets you and your
lover takes a new
name and your desk
is given to your
assistant and your
niece asks where
you've gone and
subway doors close
on your ghost
shoulders and dogs
pee on your ankles
and your last meal
remains on the plate
and your wine glass
sits full and your
napkin folded and
your best friend never
calls again and your
subscriptions expire
and the letters you
wrote combust
on my shelf and the
photos of us melt
into small puddles
along the baseboard
and your closetful
of good shoes go

stiff and your father
remembers you by
a different name
and the children
we never had stop
whispering *I love
you* in my ear.

THE THORN

I imagine him without arms.
Unable to play guitar, comb his good hair.
No more basketball. No boxing.
Forget ice cream cones, catsup-dipped French fries.
He no longer hugs his mother, or high-fives his nephews.
Cannot masturbate. I imagine his arms
on the floor. The beautiful shoulder tattoo
ripped like a shred of cloth, the nail-bitten fingers
twitching like hatchlings in a nest. His honed muscles,
deflating balloons. I imagine inside him, a thorn.
Wedged in his left lung. An unforgiving itch.
He gives it my name.

WHEN TALKING TO A DEAD GIRL
after Daphne Gottlieb

They console you over the dog.
                              Because she was alive once.
            Because you loved her and she, you.

They avoid discussing the children you won't have.
                  Refuse to speak his name.
        Careful to omit words like *ovary* and *abandon*.

No one mentions the bridge anymore.
                        No one talks of pills or razors or hair dryers.
            No one asks about the hole in your chest—

its constant spill down the front of your shirt,
                        the rancid, oozing stench.
                They ask instead, *Did you get a new dog yet?*

How did your mother die?
after Claire Kageyama-Ramakrishnan

Fly fishing on Grand Mesa.

Budweiser.

Grandpoppa's hands.

Bacardi. Cuervo. Rot-mouth.

Palm-print. Men. Fuck. Slap. Welt.
Budweiser.

On the river. On the Mesa. Alone.

My hands.

In the kitchen, at the stove.
In the prairie. The shed.
Under the blanket. In the bath.
Behind the barn. In the garden.
The cornfield. The river.

By stone. By thorn. By childbirth.

Slow. Like fog.

II

*Jezebel, which calleth herself a prophetess to teach
and to seduce my servants…and she repented not.*

—Revelation 2:20-21, *King James Bible*

LESSONS IN ALONE

On your first date, do not hand him your vagina,
polished and thirsty. Do not allow him to rub your back
or your shoulders. Do not overdrink.
When he offers to come home with you,
do not think of your ex-lover's chest. How it peeked
from behind the open neck of a pressed J. Crew button-down.
How you still masturbate to this.
Over dessert, do not think how smooth this man's thighs will be.
Do not think how lovely their dark will lay against your sheets.
Do not ask to touch during sleep, it smells like love
and you have a suitcase to unpack. You have laundry
and dishes and a dog to walk. You are busy. Stay busy.
Don't muddy your days with honey whiskey.
When the boy at the club buys you a beer, yanks you hard
from your disappearing waist, remember you owe no one.
Even if he is all your favorite music.
Keep your tongue inside your mouth.
Stop his wandering hand even if it's the only thing *good*
in New York City tonight. Say no.
When your boss suggests you meet *Nate from Accounting*
who is recently divorced, say no. Say bones break. Say love
is expensive. Remind him you have a dog and no time. You're busy.
When a friend explains, *Women have children at 45 these days, girl,*
you're good, smile. She is lying. Press her rosewater skin
under your nose. Pretend it is the skin of a newborn.
Steal this moment. She won't mind.
When Friday finally arrives and your friends leave early, let them go.
Keep your tab open. The bar has been your longest friend.
Churns out warm bodies like a factory. When the bar closes,
remember you are busy. It's time to walk the dog.
When you dress for your first date in two years, don't call it *date.*
Call it *friend.* Do not let him pay.
Share a bottle of your favorite wine, you deserve this.
When the wine makes words slippery as butter,
tell him everything you shouldn't.
Your diagnoses, how you have no insurance.

Count for him all the men you used to escape your husband.
The time you almost got a boyfriend arrested on West 4th Street.
The tryst with a colleague. Describe the miscarriage at 13.
Abortion at 25. The train engineer you fucked in Penn Station,
how his son had Leukemia. Tell how you waited six hours
at a roof party in Brooklyn one summer just to take the drummer home.
How you ran into that drummer weeks later
and couldn't recall his name. Carefully detail your unending appetite
for drink/fuck/fight, everything nasty you keep under your skin.
Do it precise. Calm.
When he runs from this quiet grenade, find the bar.
Tell yourself you did it for his sake. Besides, you're busy.
Smoke another cigarette. Take another honey whiskey.
Let it curdle your face.
You haven't been beautiful in years.

CAREFUL THE BLOOD
after Gwendolyn Brooks

Mama was a cool swathe of sad bones but
shimmied hard as a wrecking ball. I
swore I'd never move like that, never say
ass-shake or *hipswing*. Never hiss, *It's
the blues makes my tongue wet.* "She a fine
ginger," they'd say, "that arch, bend." Honest
women make dangerous property. Don't I
know what grief in a good woman can do?

Press her silk mouth to a Budweiser and
an entire pool hall would stop, lean in. I'd
be a liar to say she wasn't proud, didn't like
all those eyes reaching their long arms out to
stroke thigh, neck, each freckle. Finally to be
the spotlight, to unnerve a room. Just a
quiet country girl, legs enough to act bad.
Survive is the thing learned first. No woman
juke box without reason. Misery gotta dance, too.

This is how she mounted sorrow. Rum and
patent leather. With Bessie singing, she'd wear
floorboards down to dust. Through smoke, the
back room boys entered, all hands and brave
bearded smiles. Making prayer of stockings,
garters, the hot pearl shimmer of slick lips. Of
the bass, the thrum and thrum and night-black
wisps of sweat, flesh, and the gospel of lace.

Here I learned to move. Swore never, and
failed. It's in the blood. Mama's long strut,
hard jaw. When baby died, she counted down
the ticks of her own pulse. When papa left, the
hard in her bones hardened. Easier in the streets
when her wicked bloomed, her backhand. With
each new grief, she soured. I learned to paint

over, hide scars. Honest women last, keep on.
We make dangerous property. Careful my
hips, my bite. Careful the smile on my face.

GIRLS AND SIMPLE THINGS
for RM, MM, EH, and the writers featured at Oprah.com in "Spring
Fashion Modeled by Rising Young Poets," March 8, 2011

Once, I bought a dress in Madison, Wisconsin. A town
I've visited exactly once. The dress had black-and-white
polka dots with hot pink crinoline and a hot pink sash.

I never wore it in that town. In fact, I've worn it exactly
three times, only in New York City. Only for the most
special occasions. Only with the right boots and right bra.

The right underwear, right hairpins, lipstick, choker,
bracelets, rings, and really, it's an ordeal, this dress.
There's padding where I don't want padding. It puffs

where I don't need extra puff. It wrinkles too easily and the
sash bunches but there's pink crinoline and polka dots and it
is one of my favorite things because the day I found it, I was

with two women I love. Two women doting on themselves,
frivolous. The doting itself was permission and I am always
needing permission (to honor myself or be cold to the wretched

or ruthless to fools), so this was a day of allowances.
We had brunch then, with mimosas, and the woman
who can eat almost nothing wanted a new pair of shoes.

And the woman who laughs more loudly than everyone
wanted a new necklace. And I wanted a new dress to remind
me of the living. So we walked, thick with champagne,

firing rounds of backtalk, through the shops of Madison.
We tried jeweled sunglasses, wigs, extravagant rings,
gowns none of us could rightly afford but this was a day

of pretending. The clerk sealed someone's rhinestone heart
in a box, wrapped someone's silk cherry blossoms in tissue.
My nest of polka dots came home in a dull brown bag

where it stayed, on the closet floor, for almost two years until
another staggering woman I love moved away. For her goodbye
party, at a dive bar on the Lower East Side, I ironed, laced,

and fluffed. Wore the tallest boots, the loudest lipstick.
Knotted my hair with pins. She arrived in glitter eye shadow.
Knee-high boots. Feathers. A gown of hand-stitched sequins.

Souvenir

Somewhere in Houston a man remembers your mouth.
In Phoenix, a boy misses your hair. Chicago, your face.
Detroit, your fingernails. Somewhere, your toes,
your laughter, the tattoo on your neck. Somewhere,
a set of flannel sheets sits in the dark, hiding your stain.
A drain chokes on a stray red strand, a doorknob
quietly kisses your fingerprint. Denver is a mile
of tombstones. New York, a hive of fresh tongues.
You toss your dimples along Second Avenue
like a trail of breadcrumbs. A row of dainty landmines.

TRUISM

Last night I tangled my face
tight around Bobby Flay's lips.
Yes, Bobby Flay—master chef—
and yes, it looked as awkward
as you imagine. So much red hair
and freckle mashed together—
no telling where one cheek ended
and the other began. Blur. Like
elephant art. Everything has
happened so fast, I'm standing
in a room full of packed boxes,
dumb as a gull. Bobby is a go-
getter. Makes things happen.
Until he moved his hand up my
skirt, he didn't know. Was
surprised by the firm of my ass.
Couldn't have known how I bite.
He spotted me outside Mesa Grill
trying to hail a cab. Stuffed his
entire tongue in my mouth. Bam.
Shameful, they say. Celebrity-
kissing on the street, cameras
popping like fireworks. Bobby
promised to make me his wife.
We already named the children:
Bartleby, Hephaestus, and Thumb-
belina. He says he's loved me
since boyhood. Spent each
of his days longing. Used to park
his car in front of my apartment,
hoping for a glimpse. Left every
woman who ever loved him.
Wrote a whole book of vegetarian
recipes just for me.

THE BRAVEST THING

You notice him: tired sneakers, brown slacks, quiet green polo. Full-sleeve tattoos. Trimmed beard. Thick curls—a small patch receding from his crown. You know he is neither too young nor too old. His bag is not leather, not name-brand, his eyes are neither lost nor hungry, and you decide, yes, he is a good man. And this is your one good shot. Right here on 51st Street, feet from the mouth of a subway which might part your lives forever. You take the slow steps toward him, dodge each of the doubts hurling toward you like grenades. (What if he runs?) (Ignores me?) (What if I trip?) (Step in dog shit?) It's only five steps. Your voice is a fire alarm. *Will you marry me?*

He ashes his cigarette and smiles. *Yes.* And there you are: a clumsy bouquet in your hands, cake, guests in satin and tuxedoes. The red wine does not ruin your white dress which is white because who is actually a virgin anymore? The dinner is delicious and your friends dance and drink too much and taxis take everyone home safely, even to Brooklyn, and soon you've bought a good stroller and your clothes don't fit except the sundresses which always made you look pregnant anyway Sooner still, your daughter is two years old with perfect cheeks and auburn curls, and you are in a hospital delivering your second child and the man with the green polo and tattoos is still here, still kissing tornadoes into your soft cheeks which are softer now and you've spent half a lifetime quietly waiting for this to go wrong but it doesn't. It doesn't ever go wrong.

Now you are old and your children have children and they draw pictures for your refrigerator and the man with the sleepy sneakers is sitting beside you on a cedar porch in a good town, holding your crumpled hands and he says, *Thank you*, and you ask, *For what, love?* and he replies, *Remember the day in the city when you wore the black sundress and the candy-colored beads around your neck? Your blue nail polish was chipped and your sandals had glitter just like your hands with all the rings and I watched you and I loved you right then. And I would've taken the subway. Alone. Would've taken the train to wherever I was scheduled to go. I was a coward but you were brave. You were so brave.*

You are blushing now. Harder than you have ever blushed. You squeeze his hand, but there is only air. You look over at him but there is no one to see. You are standing on 51st Street and traffic is rushing past on Lexington, and the mouth of the subway calls you like a school bell, and he is absorbed into the flock of business suits and taxi cabs, the stir of aimless pigeons and car horns. Gone.

There Is a Dead Bison in Your Bed

You don't know how you killed it, but you're sure
it was you. There is no one else in the apartment,
except the dog who is old and filled with arthritis.

She liked the bison. Wagged her tail when it arrived,
licked its hooves, napped against its warm fur. She
knows it's dead now and she is slunk to the farthest
corner of the room, avoiding its hot stench.

The mattress is bloodsoaked. You sit at the edge
and the cool red puddles up around your thighs,
like sitting on a sopping pile of swimming towels.

Its snout is dry beneath your index finger. You rub clean
its horns, pull its lids down to hide its dark, empty eyes.
Press your ear to its mouth, hoping for some small
promise of breath, though you know this is foolish.

You cannot find the weapon. Presumably a kitchen knife,
or the hacksaw you purchased six years ago
when you were building a shelf to hold cookbooks.

But now, the hacksaw and every one of the knives
are missing. Its belly is gashed from groin to throat,
it lays face-up like a pup hoping for a tummy rub.
You cannot fathom why you'd have done this.

It was a kind, clean bison and you are a lover of animals.
It cradled you at night, bellowing lullabies. Washed your
dishes, took the dog for walks, painted your bedroom wall.

A good, sweet bison, making you laugh with its silly
grunting, and nuzzling your neck when you cried. Last you
recall, you arrived home late after too much wine. Slipped
into bed beside its heaving, matted chest and fell asleep.

Now, this. Will you have to hack it to small pieces?
Heave each leg, its massive head, wrapped in bags
down the incinerator chute? How? (The hacksaw is gone.)

You look at its soft, peaceful face, the lifeless pink
of its tongue. The cute, pointed ears still perked
as if hearing you arrive at the elevator, keys clinking.
You recall yesterday afternoon. How you rattled off

some flimsy excuse that you were unable to go picnic
in the park. You already had plans, and shouldn't
be seen in public with a bison anyway. Animal Control

might come. You might get arrested. People would stare.
You should just go it alone, you said, *enjoy the sun. Eat up
all those yummy peanut butter sandwiches you made for us.
It'll be nice,* you explained. *You can watch the kids playing*

hopscotch or run with all the dogs. Then, how you tousled
the fur on top of its head, planted a quick peck on its cheek,
and slipped out the door, saying, *I'll be home later, love.*

How you wouldn't even look it in the eyes.

FOLKLORE
for and after Eboni Hogan

As legend would have you believe, she has massacred no fewer than fourteen thousand men. Skinned each alive with her teeth. Feasted. Detangled their bones by hand, sucked the marrow, then burned what remained in an old camp stove she kept hidden under the sink.

There's tell of six hundred shades of lipstick in her medicine cabinet. Her armoire, crammed with charm bracelets strung with the toes of past lovers, and in her closet, enough pairs of lace-up shit-kicker boots to shoe an army. They say she keeps cages of live fowl (peacocks, parakeets, wild turkeys) just to have fresh-plucked feathers for her hair.

Read somewhere that she tattoos herself—sewing needles dipped into the ass-ends of ballpoint pens—because, she says, *It tickles.* They say she sometimes douses herself in bourbon, sets her dresses aflame, walks the streets of Ft. Greene at night like a beacon for young girls with broken hearts. Tells them, *Burn reminds you that you're living.* Found seventy-five spent butane lighters in a tin under her bed, a pile of charred silk stashed behind a bookcase.

Recently rumored to have migrated to the Midwest, after the epidemic of New York City cab driver mutilations abruptly ceased. Seems each refusal for Brooklyn earned a severed ear. Or tongue. They say she once twisted a driver's head clean from his shoulders, loaded his parts in the trunk, and drove herself home. Say she painted the cab mermaid-green, welded gold fins to the roof. They say you can hear his bones rattle from the back each time the car hits a pothole.

Read in the Times that she was spotted in Chicago five weeks back. Some lounge, listening to friends recite poems. When a cell phone went off, she leapt the room in one pounce, removing the culprit's eyeballs with the toothpick from her martini. She swallowed the orbs whole and calmly excused herself. Hasn't returned.

Last report, she hijacked a private jet, raced home to save some girl in Queens. Some silly young thing, playing with straight razors, slumped over in a tub with her neck opened wide. How she broke in through the window, sutured the wound, bathed the girl by hand with hot sponges, handed her a cigarette. They say the two toasted over glasses of Scotch, started plotting the murder of a Los Angeles man. Some rumor of backtalk.

COUNTRY HARD

My mama's hard as callus.
Got rot-toes. Digs dirt with her hands, pounds nails like a man.
Can work a tractor. A forklift. An 18-wheeler.
Off-road motorcycles for sport.
My mama's good with rum. Stout. Breakfasts with vodka sometimes.
Men like a woman can outdrink her man, she says.
They like a woman hard. Red hair. Men like a dirty mouth.
Some say they knew her over absinthe.
Some say they knew her over The Mesa. Over darts.
Over urinals. My mama's got gears for teeth.
Work boots and steel plates in her elbows.
She taught bone how to break.
Nurses a fat lip with ice from a glass of Jim Beam.
Kicks a man flat on his ass if he touch her again.
Don't mind that he does.
Took herself to school at 45. Got smart. Got lean. Got alone.
Moved to the mountains. Ain't nobody fish like my mama.
They say she pull a rainbow trout straight out the creek
with her hands. Seen her shoot like Marines.
Got herself an AK-47 (she won't say how) stored up top the closet.
Raised me with Grampy's .22 under my pillow.
Practiced weekends on beer cans.
My mama runs a soup kitchen without soup.
Makes fry bread and coffee thick as silt.
Marlboro Reds since she was 19, got a mouthful of yellow.
She'll spit if you look crossways once. Men like a nasty woman.
Long as she keeps good nails and stews a mean chili.
My mama's green chili is the hottest in six counties, they say.
Burn the skin off your lips before it leaves the plate.
Men like a woman with skills, she says.
Took that degree she got, started teaching boys
been kicked out of school. Ones with hit lists and bullets
in their jeans pockets. She reads them about history.
Not textbook. Manifesto.
Takes them on bounty rides to The Reservation. Prays Lakota.
Tells about Wounded Knee. Both One and Two.

Knows about policy. About America. Curses a cop in a riot.
Showed me vinegar mask for tear gas.
My mama's got tricks. Men like a woman with tricks, she says.
Like a woman with voodoo. My mama's got magic. Got flash.
Got a way with running.
She's on the mountain again. Some stretch of woods, miles deep.
Sharpening a hatchet. Conjuring a fire. Looking for a clean kill.
Catching a man the only way she know how.

JEZEBEL REVISITS THE BOOK OF KINGS
after Roger Bonair-Agard

"For the whole house of Ahab shall perish…and the dogs shall eat Jezebel…"
—*Book of Kings 2.9, King James Bible*

I wouldn't go out frayed and bleating.
Refused to racket or wail. I was a holy woman of Ba'al.
I faced the end in silk and jewels. Posture. Purple.
For this, my name means whore. Means raggedy-dance.
Means black jasmine, means sweat, stamen, ovary. Means pearl
in the wet lap of oysters. My name means ruby-lipped.
I lived in a time of men. I lived in the time of Ahab.
I am a mother of kings. I was born of hurricane and pomegranate.
Fed on the breast, I was maker of milk. I passed the stream
and the nightflowers bent to kiss me. I was evoker of hail.
Windstorm. I prodded the gods and they came. Feasted
at my table. Crowned my husband. Mine is a story of love.
Women who survive the hate of men are named harlot, witch,
Jezebel. (I still hear the dogs.) In a different century, they'd have
burned me. They'd have pressed my body to the river's floor.
I was a burning fish. Silver flakes trailed in my wake.
I was silkdance and flutter. Maker of tides. Of thorns.
Girls cowered and men flocked. I led armies
on the soft hull of my back. (A powerful woman
is simply one who has not yet died.) Flanked on all sides
by men made furious with envy. Men gone mad.
I did it for Ahab. He came to Ba'al for me.
There is nothing I wouldn't do. He wanted the castle,
I mortgaged my wrists. He asked for the crown, I slayed
the soldiers. He sought a dynasty, I gave him the globe.
Nothing less than a man would do. (Remember Helen.)
I was ear to the Prophets. Ahab's wife. Mother to Ahaziah and Jehoram.
Men raised on woman's sugar tit. Phoenicians with mouths of gold.
I was a woman with hunger. Prophecy.
Scholars name me corrupt. Name me concubine. Hussy.
Charlatan. Tainter of men. My name means wicked. Unholy.
Ahab was my only. His tongue, my tongue. His flesh, my flesh.

I was a woman in love.
They robbed me first of Ahab's breath. Then my sons.
I wasn't thrown into the pit of dogs.
I dove.

While Writing an Ode to My Lover's Hands, He Tells Me about the Revolver

for Ian John Basdeo Khadan

He dreams of revolvers. How they become
too hot to aim, pin-cock. How they melt
before he can release their dying. I cannot
see inside him. Don't know what lives there.

His hands are always unfolded before me.
Always full of gifts. Coins, milk, rose petals,
keys, answers, books, wine, praise.
He fills his mouth with impossible delusions.

Says I am large. Of the heavens, stars.
Words like *brilliant* and *unbreakable*.
His hands deserve odes written to their
every brick and nimble doing. I want

to tell you how he'd take down a building
for me with these hands, how he'd empty
a man of his blood, empty a revolver,
but he'd hesitate in my telling because

you would think him a brute. And he's right,
isn't he? You'd think him cinder-block
and pit bull. You'd picture his youth,
boys every shade of brown and bullet.

You'd guess of a ramshackle home, wonder
of his parents, if any. You'd picture clay
dust streets. Or asphalt and sirens. You'd say,
Where is Guyana on a map, anyway?

Or you'd mishear *Ghana* because we Americans
always do, as I did once, and while you might
picture it beautiful, it won't be *his* beautiful
and he cannot help but scorn over the mistaking

so I don't tell you the story. I don't tell you
he still dreams of his dogs, and coconut meat.
Don't tell of his caterpillar letters or his prayers
over the seawall. I don't tell you how he moves

graceful in the dreams, his boxer trunk dancing,
eased as ballet or Michael and his feet—how
they drape from his calves (this part is real,
though he'll never show you), angle like pointe

shoes, and he buries them in Timbs and shredded
hems on his jeans. He is six worlds in one man.
I will tell you he dreams it is me who provides
the revolver. *Always. Recurring,* he says.

My face is a barrel of stones but he calls it
freedom. Says the revolver frees him
from captors in the dreams, but I see
a woman made of gun powder,

always ticking. Always seconds away
from a struck match. How I give him
something to kill every day.
How he blesses his hands, their *able.*

LEAVING LENA
for IK, EL, JZ

Maybe she is a sex worker. Or maybe they are swingers. Or maybe it is
exactly what it is: two men on the street mauling a girl who's had more
Apple Martini than her 105 lbs. can hold. Maybe I am standing outside
with my love hoping for a cab, maybe I just can't stomach the foul
way these men's hands take and take. How they return, again and
again, to the curve of her ass. How she wobbles and swerves in her
heels. Maybe it's a trigger, this act of witness. Their laughter and
grope, how they wag their tongues. Maybe it isn't my concern. Maybe
she wants it. But maybe she doesn't, and I can't un-think this so my
chest has become a fire alarm.

It's Friday night and I am fat with glee because my brother—who is not
really my brother but my best friend, a man who could just as much
be my brother as anyone with the same heart and blood—has tonight
released his first book. Maybe we are a little loose on beer and celebration
ourselves and maybe my love and I are tired, looking for a cab home
after all this big joy, but here on the sidewalk, a girl so drunk she can't
speak. And here, these men stealing mouthfuls, filling their hands
with breast and ass. Here, not one of the twenty bystanders pausing
their good lives to consider this girl. I want to hurt these men. Maybe
for myself. Retribution, or some misguided justice, but my hunger
for it is so warm, winter vanishes and I find myself waiting—no longer
for a taxi, but an opening. It's now that she asks to sit, and they drag
her to the bench beside me and soon, I catch her name in my mouth:
Lena.

It is here that I see my love's face. He knows how I can ruin this night
if I don't *do* something. Knows how I let cowardice weigh on my bones
like a tumor, how tomorrow I will blame myself for doing nothing,
so he whispers, *Say what you need to say.* And no, I don't need his
permission, but it's important to know this won't bruise us. So her
name comes off my lips like a kiss, *Lena?* And my hand rests quiet on
her shoulder, *Lena.* Her limp neck rolls upward and she's looking in my
eyes so sweet, I know the gravity of this moment is lost on her. Right
now, I am sister, or mother, as much as I am Woman on the Street. Lena

doesn't know where she is, doesn't know why these men have so many hands.

She is dulled numb and maybe it was too many Cranberry-Vodkas but Lena isn't asking for anything. And I know I have to get her a cab home. In the soft pink of her smiling gums, I owe her this. She likes the feminine of my voice so I keep talking. I am quiet, easy, we are connecting now and if I can have just two more of her minutes—but this is where wolves become wolves. Maybe one man braces his arm against the brick to block my face. Maybe he talks to me thick with an aggression I cannot name but recognize like a hereditary sickness, the kind that turns a smooth cheekbone to blue welts; breathes a hot resentment when it hasn't been paid its due for the overpriced risotto or the extra bottle of wine. The kind that reeks of bourbon and entitlement. Maybe it is how hard I am ignoring him. How little he matters. Maybe it's because I, too, am a woman, and what audacity for me to interrupt his good fun.

The sneer on his face is turning rancid, his words go hostile and soon, my love takes offense because this is no gentleman, and all the while, Lena, with her glossy lips. I'm asking how she feels. If she knows where she is, does she want to go home, can I get her a cab. *Lena, listen, I just want to make sure*—but then there's a fist. Someone is cursing, and now, I'm about to swing on a man for my love and I drop my bag so I can swing because this is happening. Right now, this is real. There are men and fists and here, now, they're dragging Lena away, and someone's holding me back and maybe I'm screaming. Maybe I'm saying, *No, Lena.* Maybe I'm yelling at someone to let me go, to let Lena go. *Don't let them take her!* I'm screaming now. *I know what they'll do! I know what they'll do! I know, I know!* And maybe I begin to sob.

Maybe this is when I realize my bag is gone. Maybe this is when I punch the side window. Maybe I knock over a row of chairs. Maybe now my friends are fevered too because they spot a man running across Bowery with a lady's handbag. My bag. Now my love and our boys are a tornado of racing boots but I don't know this. I'm inside breaking chairs, and I don't know they are in chase. Don't know it is one of Lena's men running away with my bag, don't know my friends are chasing him down 1st Street. Don't know he isn't fast enough, that they snatch back the bag but my love is angry now and this man is getting his due. I don't know that my love is landing fist after fist until the man wriggles loose, then is caught again and tries to fight but maybe he is white and I'll tell you here that my friends are brown. I'm not there to hear one of them say, *Stop. Let him go. We got her bag and dude is white and we all know how this looks.*

I don't know then how they hush, listen for sirens, scan the block for police; how then, instead, Lena. Here now, Lena, wobbling, arm-in-arm with the first of her men. Maybe she's delusional, claiming my bag is her bag. Maybe she is so fogged by martini and brutes she starts claiming my things are her things. My books, her books—even the one inscribed to *Jeanann, my sister,* by the brother who is not my brother. Maybe now her man understands. Sees his broken boy and a sidewalk full of brown men and a bag filled with another woman's living and Lena, fiery, drunk enough to lie for these men despite everything. Maybe now he knows this was never a game, and I'm not there to hear him curse at Lena. To hear his, *Shut-the-fuck-up!* echo low and cold off the asphalt. I'm not there to watch Lena's eyes cloud over as the men I love like brothers turn their backs.

WHY YOU CRY AT THE END OF HER LIFE

Sure, the dog is old and you have been waiting.
You're not a fool and she is not mythological.

This is life. And life gets tired and filled
with heart disease. Life loses all her muscle mass

and must be carried up the stairs. Life can't stand up
for long, and lets her food rot in the bowl until flies arrive.

Life lays down, always. Patches of fur
coming off in clumps. Life snivels, snots, hacks

and sometimes sneezes on your feet. Life is a dog.
And it doesn't even matter if she is a good dog

(she is) or a kind dog (she is) or a pretty dog (she is)
or an expensive dog (she isn't). What matters now,

as she is leaving you day by dreadful day, slow and sad
as a person who shits his thighs or a hip that crumbles

just for walking—the reason you kneel on the floor
for hours and kiss her hot breath, and look

into her fogging grey eyes; what matters is not
the sorry mess of animal you've got laid up

in a sling on your living room floor, spitting up
antibiotics, slobbering and leaking piss—what matters here

is the night she fought those men. Her bark and panic,
her yelp beneath their boots, the snarl she gave.

The stubborn growl. The refusal. It is how she *tried*.
You, naked and beaten. And she, the fighter.

BRIDGE SONG
to Angel Nafis

These men. They come hard. Fast.
Grains of sand in a windstorm. Not been
myself lately. Been jumping rivers,

collecting knives. Sedatives. Been fishing
with my tongue in the throats of men.
Find dead things stashed between their teeth.

I opened my shirt. My chest. Opened doors,
windows. Wrists, thighs. I've said it honest
as I know how: *This is me. This is all.*

*Isn't much. I am heart and breath and skin
and bleed. Sometimes tornado, sometimes
lullaby.* They take, Angel. They take.

They say too much. Words made
from lead. *Marriage. Children. Today.
Love. Ready. Yes.* Why do they leave?

Been ignored so hard my skin turned
to wood. My tongue, salt. They got me:
forgotten jewelry in a drawer, ornaments

in boxes, old trophy in a basement. *Just lay
in those sheets, woman. Just lay quiet.
I'll get to you after you repent. Once*

you hate yourself hard enough. When I
doused the rafters in kerosene and went in
with the blowtorch, after the corpses

were dragged out and buried proper,
I thought staying right meant staying honest.
Just be truth and you can't get hurt, right?

Said, *A girl made of splinters isn't built
for love.* But they tried, anyway. They tried.
And turns out, I can. I can love hard

as shrapnel. So hard I melt skin. There was
a night in the sheets—the sheets that once
were his—another man's heat and me,

a dogpile of convulsion, lurch and moan.
I sobbed because he was gone, and that man
held me, Angel. Held me like a father holds

rage, arms tight across as lifejacket.
Shuddered like that 'til daybreak.
He whispered, *I want this wreckage.*

Now, his mouth is full. Gold strands of hair.
Got condoms. Got limos. Got whiskey
and football and steak to fry.

He walked me in the rain. Sweet-talked me
with daisies. Talked me off that bridge.
Made me laugh. Laugh—even when the city

and my face were on fire. I sink
to my sheets. It's always the sheets.
The soak and stain of old linen.

Lay myself flat, spread myself thin.
Flatten hips and breasts, roll outward
like a layer of seeping cream.

Get thin and thin and thin. Reach for
the edges of the mattress, pray to be thin
as paper, thin as invisible. Thin as never.

It's so empty here. Always empty.
Always fighting some man in the street.
Always fighting. No one wants the wreckage,

Angel. No one strong enough. I'm afraid
of the river. Afraid it's going to start calling
again. Afraid I'll wake up tomorrow

and my front door will open directly
to the mouth of that bridge. I'm afraid
of the fish. How their tails will pull me under.

Afraid of the boats, their propellers,
life vests. I'm afraid of the corpses,
all the girls never found.

Afraid of the men, Angel.
How they tug at the meat.
How sharp their teeth.

III

Thou art Kali...the Beginning of all,
Creatrix, Protectress, and Destructress

—Shiva, *Mahanirvana Tantra*

Wherein the Author Provides Footnotes and Bibliographic Citation for the First Stanza Drafted after a Significant and Dangerous Depression Incurred upon Being Referenced as a "Hack" Both by Individuals Unknown to the Author and by Individuals Whom the Author Had Previously Considered Friends (*) (†) (‡) (§)

by 35[1], when madness[2] had overcome her[3]; when her body[4]
sloshed[5] like[6] rubbery meat[7] in the softest swells
of armsag[8] and stomach fold[9];
when the night brought[10] marching ants[11] to her[12] pillow[13]
and[14] wailing[15] teapots[16] swarmed in the kitchen[17];
when the cannibals came[18] wearing eyeliner and capped teeth[19];
when the flock of birds erupted from her throat[20],
leaving her mouth a clog[21] of feathers[22],
she paced the apartment[23], a fury[24]. a yowling beast[25].
caged rhinoceros[26], severed horn[27] in its bloody[28] maw[29, 30]. (‖)

---

[1] "by 35" | References author's own age. Mercy Hospital, Denver, Colorado, March 1974.

[2] "madness" | Term used to reference mental illness, specifically within the manic phase of Manic Depression.

[3] "had overcome her" | Happenstance of exact quotation, discovered after drafting stanza: Yeats, *On Baile's Strand,* Character: Fool, Page 23.

[4] "when her body" | Happenstance of exact quotation, discovered after drafting stanza. Chivers, "Ceratioid Anglerfish," Line 24.

[5] "her body sloshed" | Similar use of verb root, discovered after drafting stanza: "The train sloshes." McDaniel, "St. Theresa of the 6," Line 3. (Formula: [article/pronoun] [noun] slosh/es/ed.)

[6] "like" | Colloquialism in Southern California, most American High Schools, and various Skateboard Parks across the United States, often used to fill silence in conversation, replacing the more common terms, "uh" or "um." Also used in employment of similes, meaning "similar." Preposition.

[7] "rubbery meat" | The quality of overcooked flesh. Hirsh, "Microwaves no longer make rubbery meat."

[8] "armsag" | Term fabricated by author. Concept credit: 1. "sweatdrop." Bonair-

Agard, "the tragicomedy of the black boy blues or a hip-hop nigretto or the boy became black at JFK," Stanza 7, Line 9. 2. "gumpopper." Smith, "Little Poetry," Line 1. 3. "Alchemistical." Sands, "Party and Bullshit," Stanza 10, Line 2.

[9] "in the softest swells of armsag and stomach fold" | Line structure reminiscent of "in the darkest folds of the mouth." Falkner, "My Father's Family," Line 47. (Formula: in the [this]est [something] of [something else].)

[10] "the night brought" | Happenstance of thematic similarity (things that happen at night; nighttime behaviors; nighttime fears), discovered after drafting stanza. Thomas, "Now Comes the Night," audio.

[11] "marching ants" | Animation technique in computer graphics, popularized by programs such as MacPaint and Adobe Photoshop.

[12] "her" | References author's ownership of the object within the statement (common sleeping tool: The Pillow). Definition: possessive case of "she." Pronoun.

[13] "when the night brought marching ants to her pillow" | Reference to phobias commonly associated with various mental illnesses/anxiety disorders. Myrmecophobia: fear of ants; Noctiphobia: fear of night.

[14] "and" | Happenstance of exact quotation, discovered after drafting stanza. Holy Bible, "Genesis 1:1." Since its appearance in the aforementioned publication, the term has become a colloquialism among English speaking individuals. Definition: "also" or "plus." Conjunction.

[15] "wailing" | Author here draws a parallel between the whistle of a heated tea kettle and the sound commonly emitted during the act of weeping. Definition: prolonged, inarticulate, mournful cry. Verb.

[16] "teapots" | An amalgamation of "teacup[1]" and "honeypot[2]" (1. Mojgani, "biography," Para. 3, Line 2.) (2a. Milne, Winnie-the-Pooh, Character: Pooh. Object of Pooh's affection.) (2b. McKibbens, "Grizzly," audio.)

[17] "wailing teapots swarmed in the kitchen" | Reference to the author's method self-consoling during bouts of insomnia[1] through the routine of preparing tea. (1. "Insomnia" | Sleep disorder with varied causes, most commonly, stress.)

[18] "the cannibals came" | References the cannibals who appear in "beautiful: a legend." Verlee, "beautiful: a legend," Part 2, Stanza 6, Line 3.

[19] "wearing eyeliner and capped teeth" | References eHow.com article, "How to Make a Jack Sparrow[1] Costume." (1. Character from Pirates of the Caribbean: Curse of the Black Pearl.)

[20] "the flock of birds erupted from her throat" | References artwork[1] by Tyson Schroeder. (1. Artwork for the cover of Racing Hummingbirds[2].) (2. Book titled after the poem, "racing hummingbirds[3].") (3. Poem written in reference to author's bouts of mania[4].) (4. Mania is a function of Manic Depression.)

[21] "clog" | Emergency room physician used this term in specific reference to a mysterious collection of dead cells in an artery in the arm of the author's father, meaning "obstruction." Quote: Dr. Allen, PhD., Littleton Adventist Hospital, December, 2009.

[22] "leaving her mouth a clog of feathers" | Author took liberty to employ logic following preceding phrase. (No citation.)

[23] "she paced the apartment" | Happenstance of exact quotation, discovered after drafting stanza. Turney, Love Has Many Faces, Chap. II, Para. 2, Line 2.

[24] "fury" | References rage. Rage is a function of Manic Depression.

[25] "yowling beast" | Happenstance of exact quotation, discovered after drafting stanza. Michael Rumaker's "Later Thoughts on 'Howl'" as detailed by Hyde, On the Poetry

of Allen Ginsberg (Under Discussion), Page 40.

[26] "she paced the apartment, a fury. a yowling beast. caged rhinoceros" | Line structure reminiscent of the common simile, "paced the floor like a caged animal." References animal psychology, particularly that of caged animals.

[27] "rhinoceros, severed horn" | Metaphorical[1] reference to the act of destroying a creature for the base greed of obtaining its most unique attribute or asset. Specific reference to the species' endangered status due to poaching for removal of the horn. (1. "metaphor" | English term meaning "linguistic symbol." Noun.)

[28] "bloody" | Upon removal of body parts, animals typically bleed. Also known as "hemorrhage."

[29] "maw" | Happenstance of exact quotation, discovered after drafting stanza. 1. Alighieri, "Inferno," Page 39, Line 12. 2. Smith, "Siblings," Line 20. 3. Menchavez, "Hot, or Why I Boogie," Line 5.

[30] "severed horn in its bloody maw" | Metaphorical reference to self-destructive behavior[1]. (1. "self-destructive behavior" | References a coping mechanism common during episodes of depression. Depression is a function of Manic Depression.)

---

*Footnoted poem concept credit (samples): 1. Tolson, "E. & O. E." 2. Gottlieb, *selected poems.* 3. Fabri, "The Word-Lover's Miscarriage."

† Absurdist elongated title style (samples): 1. Wordsworth, "Lines Left upon a Seat in a Yew-Tree Which Stands Near the Lake of Esthwaite, on a Desolate Part of the Shore, Yet Commanding a Beautiful Prospect." 2. Rosal, "On Our Long Road Trip Home I Don't Ask My Friend If He Thinks His Youngest Daughter Might Be Someone Else's Kid." 3. Aptowicz, "In Lieu of Her Boyfriend Writing Any New Poetry, the Author Critiques the Four Line Song She Heard Him Spontaneously Create While Drunkenly Walking Up Their Apartment Building's Stairwell."

‡ Use of "Author" within poem title as self-aware parody concept credit (samples): 1. McKibbens, "Finally, The Author Gets Personal." 2. Aptowicz, "In Lieu of Her Boyfriend Writing Any New Poetry, the Author Critiques the Four Line Song She Heard Him Spontaneously Create While Drunkenly Walking Up Their Apartment Building's Stairwell."

§ Title case title format. "Principles of Headline-Style Capitalization," *The Chicago Manual of Style, 16th Edition.*

¿ Punctuation without capitalization poem format (samples): 1. Smith, "What Men Do With Their Mouths." 2. McConnell, "dream about transference as a reasonable excuse." 3. Coval, "Waking Up / In Chicago."

Bibliography

Alighieri, Dante. "Inferno." In *The Divine Comedy.* Circa 1310. Translated by Rev. H. F. Cary. Kessinger Publishing, 2004.

Aptowicz, Cristin O'Keefe. "In Lieu of Her Boyfriend Writing Any New Poetry, the Author Critiques the Four Line Song She Heard Him Spontaneously Create While Drunkenly Walking Up Their Apartment Building's Stairwell." In *Everything is Everything*. Write Bloody Publishing, 2010.

Bonair-Agard, Roger. "the tragicomedy of the black boy blues or a hip-hop nigretto or the boy became black at JFK." In *Gully*. Cypher Books, 2010.

Chivers, Tom. "Ceratioid Anglerfish." *insert poem here,* February 15, 2007. http://insertpoemhere.blogspot.com/2007/02/ceratioid-anglerfish.html.

Coval, Kevin. "Waking Up / In Chicago." *Everyday People.* EM Press, 2008.

eHow Contributior. "How to Make a Jack Sparrow Costume." *eHow.com.* http://www.ehow.com/how_2061149_make-jack-sparrow-costume.html.

Elliott, Ted, and Terry Rossio. *Pirates of the Caribbean: Curse of the Black Pearl.* Walt Disney Pictures, 2003.

Fabri, Erica. "The Word-Lover's Miscarriage." In *Dialect of a Skirt*. Hanging Loose Press, 2009.

Falkner, Adam. "My Father's Family." *The ESU Review.* University of Pennsylvania Press, 2009.

Gottlieb, Daphne. *Kissing Dead Girls.* Soft Skull Press, 2008.

Hirsh, J.M. "Microwaves no longer make rubbery meat." *Lubbock Avalanch-Journal,* August 13, 2008. http://www.lubbockonline.com/stories/081308/liv_317987731.shtml.

Holy Bible. "Genesis." *Holy Bible: King James Version.* Thomas Nelson, 2002.

Hyde, Lewis, editor. *On the Poetry of Allen Ginsberg (Under Discussion).* University of Michigan Press, 1985.

Jameson, Kay Redfield. *An Unquiet Mind: A Memoir of Moods and Madness.* Vintage Books, division of Random House, Inc., 1995.

Merriam-Webster Editorial Staff. *Merriam-Webster's Collegiate Dictionary: 11th Edition.* Encyclopedia Britannica, 2003.

McConnell, Marty. "dream about transference as a reasonable excuse." *Boxcar Poetry Review,* January, 2007. http://www.boxcarpoetry.com/006/mcconnell_marty_002.html.

McDaniel, Jeffrey. "St. Theresa of the 6." In *The Endarkenment.* University of Pittsburgh Press, 2008.

McKibbens, Rachel. "Finally, The Author Gets Personal." In *Pink Elephant.* Cypher Books, 2009.

—"Grizzly," audio. *Ragazine.cc: Poetry Out Loud,* 2009. http://ragazine.cc/wp-content/uploads/2009/10/Grizzly.mp3

Menchavez, Ed. "Hot, or Why I Boogie." In *Still, Weightless an Outlaw Star.* Self-published, 2010.

Milne, A.A. *Winnie-the-Pooh.* Methuen & Co. Ltd., 1926.

Mojgani, Anis. "Biography." *LivePoets.com,* 2008. http://www.livepoets.com/poet.aspx?id=225.

National Institute of Mental Health Staff. "Anxiety Disorders. Phobias." *National Institute of Mental Health,* 2010. http://www.nimh.nih.gov/health/publications/anxiety-disorders/specific-phobias.shtml.

Newkirk, Ingrid. *Free the Animals: The Story of the Animal Liberation Front.* Lantern Books, 2000.

PBS: Nature Staff Writer. "Rhino Horn Use: Fact vs. Fiction." *PBS: Nature,* August 20, 2010.

http://www.pbs.org/wnet/nature/episodes/rhinoceros/rhino-horn-use-fact-vs-fiction/1178.

Rosal, Patrick. "On Our Long Road Trip Home I Don't Ask My Friend If He Thinks His Youngest Daughter Might Be Someone Else's Kid." In *My American Kundiman*. Peresa Books, 2006.

Sands, Jon. "Party and Bullshit." *The New Clean*. Write Bloody Publishing, 2011.

Scully, Matthew. *Dominion: The Power of Man, the Suffering of Animals, and the Call to Mercy*. St. Martin's Press, 2002.

Smith, Patricia. "Little Poetry." In *Teahouse of the Almighty*. Coffee House Press, 2006.

—"What Men Do With Their Mouths." In *Teahouse of the Almighty*. Coffee House Press, 2006.

—"Siblings." In *Blood Dazzler*. Coffee House Press, 2008.

Thomas, Rob. "Now Comes the Night," audio. *Something to Be*. Atlantic Recording Corporation, 2005.

Tolson, Melvin. "E. & O. E." *Poetry*, 1951.

Turney, Denise. *Love Has Many Faces*. Chistell Publishing, 2000.

University of Chicago Press Staff. *The Chicago Manual of Style, 16th Edition*. University of Chicago Press, 2010.

Verlee, Jeanann. "beautiful: a legend." In *Racing Hummingbirds*. Write Bloody Publishing, 2010.

Wikipedia. "Bleeding." 2010. http://en.wikipedia.org/wiki/Bleeding.

— "Insomnia." 2010. http://en.wikipedia.org/wiki/Insomnia.

— "Marching ants." 2010. http://en.wikipedia.org/wiki/Marching_ants

— "Rhinoceros horn." 2010. http://en.wikipedia.org/wiki/Rhinoceros#Horns.

Wordsworth, William. "Lines Left upon a Seat in a Yew-Tree Which Stands Near the Lake of Esthwaite, on a Desolate Part of the Shore, Yet Commanding a Beautiful Prospect," 1795. Reprinted in *Lyrical Ballads*. Penguin Books, 1999.

Yeats, W.B. *On Baile's Strand*. Dun Emer Press, 1903.

THE VOICES

I never believed in voices. Ian's mad.
Thought it was Psychology's answer

to the inexplicable experience of schizophrenics.
Eva resents you. I've read detail of the way such voices
communicate to the sufferer. Paul will never

forgive you. Nate doesn't believe you. I understood
the tortured mind hears voices audibly. In the way

one hears noises at night: beams and bits of dust
settling in a quiet room. William's lying.
Maggie thinks you're a coward. Your father

will be disgusted. You are disgusting. The audible
way wind taps at windows, or unseen animals

rustle leaves in the dark: sound. He left because you're pathetic.
Because you're ugly. You're ugly. You're fat. You're old.
Look at your hair. Your teeth are rotting. Your gums are receding.

You'll never be pretty. You'll never have children. You'll never
be worthy. I deemed such voices came as different individuals,

each with its own distinct personality. Brian's lying. Your mother isn't
speaking to you. Call your mother. Each voice emerging
with its own pitch, timbre, gender, ethnicity. The team hates your work.

They're laughing at you. The committee wants you to resign.
The committee doesn't believe you. Your father doesn't believe

you. No one believes you. The common inference
is that during a psychotic break, an increasing number
of these distinct voices begin communicating Mike is dead.

to the sufferer at an ever-quickening speed Linda is angry. wherein
the sound grows so loud and the information so overbearing,

the sufferer Your mother hates you. can no longer connect with tangible,
real-world senses. It's over. You failed. It's happening. Bill wants you fired.
Marc thinks you're a liar. They think you're a coward. Coward.

You're pathetic. You should die. Further, it is understood
that during such a break the culminating voices

become threatening and violent in nature. Everyone knows.
Alan thinks you're lazy. Wes hates you. Fuck you.
They think you're a fraud. The receptionist is listening.

Mallory thinks you're weak. Call her. No. You are a bad person.
Your dog is dying because you are a bad person. Nobody likes you.

Everyone is lying. They think you're a hack. You bitch. This is it.
You are gone. There's no going back. They're watching. You slut.
Look what you've done. You ruined everything. You're okay.

Whore. You're okay. You're okay. Useless cunt. You're okay.
You're okay. You're okay. Die. You're okay. You're okay.

You. Are. Okay. You should die. You're okay. You're okay.
You're okay. You're okay. It was my understanding that voices
come audible as coins dropped to the floor, a dog's bark.

I understood that when my time came, I would hear voices.

Manic

The crack and hiss, her streaks

                                 in the dark: sparkler tails,
phoenix wings.

              Bare feet slap
                   the pavement, flames lick

each lover's face. She darts,
                      circles between distractions.

The conversation she cannot
finish, again.
                        A collection
                        of dishes, soda cans,
unanswered phone calls.

                  She is the redheaded breeze on your face.

        She is the movement,
                    the hum and stir.

The cut and fury.   Tornado,
                  iron-fanged wrath.

She is the fistful of rings,   the pile of glass
        after the steel tip of a boot.

                  This is how the mind frays.
How a mad girl pops and sizzles.

HEREDITARY

I have a twitch sometimes. I keep my left eye open in my sleep.
That hole in the bathroom door was not me.
The scar on my forearm, an accident. Burst vessel in my eye,
the blackened palms, tire marks on I-25—not me.
The patch of scalp, doorknob through a bedroom wall,
knife wound across the cabinet's face, the sixth time
we replaced a set of wine glasses, TV hurled like a dodge ball,
the cell phone torn in half—I am not crazy, this is just Thursday.
I live alone, pay rent and taxes. I cook and fold laundry.
There are no monsters here; I don't see ghosts.
I did not sleep with a razor in my teeth last night.
I do not keep count of my 16-year pill collection.
Haven't had a drink in 43 hours. I have four alarm clocks
and too many shoes. This morning, I ripped open a tin can
with my own hands, cursed a man at the bagel cart. One time,
I said, *Ma, calm down,* and she slapped me so hard I forgot her name.

BRAWLER

I was born of the fist. The hot Irish temper.
Trailer parks. Pabst Blue Ribbon. Men in work boots,
crusted wifebeaters. Fire ants. Weevils. Moth wings on window sills.
Rheumatic fever, scoliosis, lengthwise cesarean scars.
I was born of the hunt. Antlers and tanned hides.
Antelope, elk, white-tailed deer. Meat and bone.
Jack Daniels, Johnnie Walker, Jim Beam.
Born of thistle. Rattlesnakes. Flat bed pickup trucks. Asphalt.
Murals on cinder-block walls. Vandals and graffiti.
Smoking weed in the girls bathroom, the alley behind the dumpster,
out the library window. Backseat, abandoned warehouse,
basketball court. Born of weed. Acid. Paint thinner. Rail yards.
Sucking homeless dick for a nip of vodka.
Homeless. Runaway. Welt. *Shut your face and take it.*
Born of Marlboro Reds, rum-and-Coke, adultery. Rolling pins.
Flour-dusted aprons. Green pork fat chili and hot peppers. Tequila.
Shaved pussy. Thigh-highs. Pink mohawk. Steel toes.
Bar fight. Cut lip. Face-grind. Elbow-to-sternum. Wrist-pin.
I am from *no.* From *please.* From *stop. Hush. Hiss. I-will-cut-you.*
Born of morning glories and dirt yards. Splinter, oil pan, rusted engine.
I was born of hand-me-down, foreclosure notice, *electric company*
shut off the power. Budweiser and wiskerin's. Where creek is *crik,*
wash is *warsh,* and no one can pronounce *February.*
Born of buckshot. Cannon fire. Smooth aim. Bull's-eyes
and beer can crates. From *Push, woman! Don't be a sissy.*
From *I didn't raise some cupcake, now quit yer cryin'*
or I'll give you something to cry about.
I'm from having something to cry about but biting down hard—
'til lip bleeds salt through the teeth. Wrench and gear and gristle.
Born of hillbilly backwoods, knitted doilies, tobacco stains.
Gridlock traffic. Gang fight. Homicide. "The Projects."
Mustard-and-cracker sandwiches *'til a paycheck comes through.*
Reused tinfoil, washable diapers, coffee tins full of pennies.
Born of *when the bottle won't break, use your hands.*
I'm from *use your hands. Sound it out. Try harder. Never settle.*
Born of callus. Hammer. Knuckle scar. Flesh wound.

Working hands. I was born of working hands. *Keep swinging.*
Kick hard and leave scars. Born of curse. Diesel fuel. Powder keg.
Move, rise, gallop. Never give up. Never give up. Never give up.
Over my dead body. I dare you.

INSOMNIA

"Edit this." "Answer this." "Help me on this." "Organize this."
"Do it for free." "Arrange this." "Coordinate this." "For free."
"For the community." "For the sense of accomplishment."
"Do it for the girls." "For the next generation." "For me."
"The laundry has really piled up." "Dishes too." "Don't stress."
"Read my manuscript." "Mine, too." "Give me your feedback."
"Do me a solid." "Show up." "Don't be late." "Leave work early."
"New series. No pay." "Need you. No pay." "Come to my show."
"My reading." "My dinner." "My birthday." "My show."
"My show." "Smile." "Don't stress." "Why weren't you there?"
"Selfish." "It's always about you." "Don't be so emotional."
"Shh." "Let it go." "Edit this." "Call me." "Payment is late."
"Report's late." "Project's late." "Gig for no pay." "60/40 split."
"You're so lucky." "You've got it all." "What's to worry about?"
"Schedule this." "Cancel this." "Book it." "Reschedule." "Smile."
"You've really let yourself go." "There's a hole in your sweater."
"Your coat." "Stain on your scarf." "You need a manicure."
"Make time." "Don't stress." "What's to stress about?"
"You brought this on yourself." "Get over it." "Get over him."
"Move on." "Forgive." "Get past it." "Edit this?" "Review this?"
"No pay." "Feature. No pay." "Feature. Pay your own admission."
"Why don't you return my calls?" "My texts?" "Voicemail's full."
"Place is a wreck." "Get it together." "Need you out of town."
"Why aren't you touring?" "Quit your job." "Rent's due."
"Don't panic." "You're so sensitive." "Believe in yourself."
"Take some time for yourself." "I need you." "I never see you."
"What do you mean, 'can't sleep?'" "Don't stress." "Finish this."
"Late on this." "Where's that book I loaned you?" "Get to it."
"Get to work." "Get ready." "Need you early." "Need you late."
"Need you on this." "Help me on this." "Need your advice."
"Read my manuscript yet?" "Make time." "What's next for you?"
"When're you getting an MFA?" "Start writing that show yet?"
"Apply for that residency yet?" "Where's your next manuscript?"
"Can I send my thesis?" "My project?" "My poem?" "Edit this."
"Call me." "I'm in town tonight." "This weekend." "Make time."
"Need it now." "Need your opinion." "Call me back." "Got a minute?"

WAKING KALI

A siren erupts in the dark.
                    It is her throat.
The apartment is empty.
                    She lurches, swoops.
        Aims for things that are not real.
Her body is a fist.
                    Her heart,
            a twelve-cylinder engine.
She writhes and folds.
                    Plants bruises into her breastbone,
        her temples, her thighs.
She strikes the doorframe.
                    The counter, windowsill.
Thunders the hardwood in hot circles,
                    pistons in her ankles.
Prays to be made of stone.

Good Girl

Every morning I sit at the kitchen table over a tall glass of water swallowing pills. (So my hands won't shake.) (So my heart won't race.) (So my face won't thaw.) (So my blood won't mold.) (So the voices won't scream.) (So I don't reach for knives.) (So I keep out of the oven.) (So I eat every morsel.) (So the wine goes bitter.) (So I remember the laundry.) (So I remember to call.) (So I remember the name of each pill.) (So I remember the name of each sickness.) (So I keep my hands inside my hands.) (So the city won't rattle.) (So I don't weep on the bus.) (So I don't wander the guardrail.) (So the flashbacks go quiet.) (So the insomnia sleeps.) (So I don't jump at car horns.) (So I don't jump at cat-calls.) (So I don't jump a bridge.) (So I don't twitch.) (So I don't riot.) (So I don't slit a strange man's throat.)

The Mania Speaks

You clumsy bootlegger. Little daffodil.
I watered you with an ocean & you plucked one little vein?
Downed a couple bottles of pills & got yourself carted off to the ER?
I gifted you the will of gunpowder, a matchstick tongue,
& all you managed was a shredded sweater & a police warning?
You should be legend by now.
Girl in an orange jumpsuit, a headline.
I built you from the purest napalm, fed you wine & bourbon.
Preened you in the dark, hammered lullabies into your thin skull.
I painted over the walls, wrote the poems.
I shook your goddamn boots. Now you want out?
Think you'll wrestle me out of you with prescriptions?
A good man's good love & some breathing exercises?
You think I can't tame *that?* I always come home. Always.
Ravenous. Loaded. You know better than anybody:
I'm bigger than God.

THE SMALLEST GIRL

You notice your breasts have dropped a cup size.
Two. The toenails you clipped two weeks ago

haven't grown back. The rings you usually wear
slip straight off your fingers. Your teeth are nubs

the size of a baby's. Every dress drops from your shoulders
to a useless heap at your ankles. You slurp pudding

from straws because spoons are too wide for your mouth.
You take showers in the sink, drink wine from thimbles.

Perch atop overturned teacups, shouting to be heard
in ordinary conversations. You teach the dog to hail cabs,

sit shotgun on top of the meter. Hitch rides beneath shoelaces,
inside coin purses, along the loops of ladies' earrings.

Write emails by leaping from one key to the next.
You miss, fall into the crevice between the j and the k.

Your friends have stopped calling.
Some rumor you moved away.

HOW DID THE AUTHOR DIE?
after Claire Kageyama-Ramakrishnan and Ross Gay

Over the George Washington Bridge.

Budweiser.

Mama's hands.

Jameson. Cuervo. Rot-mouth.

Palm-print. Men. Fuck. Slap. Welt.
Budweiser.

On the river. On the streets. Alone.

Her own hands.

In the kitchen, at the stove.
In the alley. The shed.
Under the blanket. In the bath.
Behind the tracks. On the bar.
The stage. The river.

By stone. By thorn. By childbirth.

Slow. Like fog.

I Imagined It Nude, or in a Black Dress

I didn't know I was dressing for dying.
That day was for mimosas. For late-summer
pearls of sweat and my lover's good hands. Family.
I dressed at noon. Polka dots, pink ribbons.
Boots. My favorite rings. A smile, finally.
Couldn't imagine the cold blue girl pinned
between the folds, midnight's blood on the hem.

Tracing Wrist Scars

I used to keep exquisite potted plants.
Now, just pots of dirt.
My friend Meghann keeps pots of dirt.
One with a ceramic hand creeping out,
another, a foot. Funny, the things we covet.
I only learned to begin wanting again
recently. I don't know where to place my wants.
How to justify them, or actually obtain.
It isn't fair to want things
after trying to give everything away.
The wine isn't fair, the overpriced penne.
Paycheck, new boot laces, a night out for music
or poetry or beer. This guilt.
Wanting a day of sun. Or even rain.
Things that racket and wail, things that shimmy
or sit quietly on a windowsill.
Shameful, I think, to covet a tattoo
or philosophical conversation.
A book, a trinket. A new poem. A pulse.

The Sick Is an Ocean

Why is fire the only metaphor I have for all this dying?
Who feeds the dogs when I end? Where have all the rivers gone?
When did I learn to float? I cut my finger on a piece of tin
in the office kitchen. I have an office. I have appointments. Plans.
I've cut my finger and don't care to find a Band-Aid.
This is the office kitchen and I have rent to pay. What of my privilege?
I have coffee and too many shoes. A bank account. Body lotion
and dental floss. What of the invisible sick?
Nothing but a river will do. What if I lose the map?
How will I meet the bridge? What if I never find my hands?
Why does the cut clot? Where does a sedative go to die?
I keep secrets in obvious places. Stole another box of razors.
Hide sleeping pills in the underwear drawer. A new end
wakes me every morning. How far is four stories?
What if I crush a pigeon? Where does guilt go? I have all this privilege
and I'm always trying to leave. There's leftover chicken
in the office fridge. I'm vegetarian so I give it to Lupe
who cleans the office and has two little boys.
What would Lupe do if I ended here? Why all this blood?
Who can show me where I keep my bed? Who will love my father
when I'm gone? Who will clean this goddamned kitchen?
Red fingerprints, everywhere.

HOME

You want your father who is not here
and who wouldn't be—not here, in New York,
on a night after too much dark rum; a night

after a girlfriend two thousand miles away
gives birth to a three-pound girl now roped

and wired inside a plastic box. Not here,
a night where you drop to the floor in a stairwell
sobbing over the matter-of-fact-ness of the girl

and her tubes and her mama's, *Just happy everyone
made it through,* and the scarring hot scald

of your own fractured childlessness. You want
your father. Here. Want him to tell you you're smart
and beautiful and worth something to someone.

To tell you the girl will survive. That you will survive.
That the boy who left you on the side of the road

wasn't real. That none of this is real, and it hits you
here, on the floor, breaking into bullets: it is too late.
This stairwell, this handrail. New York City wailing

outside, while hurricane Irene, who is really a small
wet whisper, tells you, *Hush—sit on the floor.* Now.

This floor. This rum. This face, yours, rancid
as old cream. You want your dead heart to be a
hummingbird. Or jet fuel. You want a roadmap.

You want your father. You want to kiss the lips
of a bridge. You want saltines smeared with mustard

like mama used to pack in your Muppets lunchbox.
You want your mama. No, you want the lunch box
and the boy named Jonathan who made you blush.

Jonathan, before he liked the other girl. You want
the boy named Miguel or Graham or Jon or Robert

or Dennis, before he liked the other girl. Before
you fought for him with yes/no/maybe notes,
or poems with too many teeth. Before you fought.

Before you knew how to hurl a fist or regret a curse.
Before you learned all the things you could break

with your hands. Before you knew the control
of a baseball bat or a tire iron or a .9 millimeter.
Before you knew the power of an uncorked bottle,

a glass of rum, a spent tube of Xanax. Before they
bound you with telephone cords, before they drugged

you limp and gaping, before the boy with cheap poems
and cocaine rage pried you open in your sleep.
Before the night after too much wine, after a night

after too much whiskey, after a night after too much rum,
before the night—this night—here, on the stairs

with the wind rattling the door while your girl's girl
is trying not to die and you are trying not to die
and all you want is your father. Or a future. Or a river.

Finally I Allow Him the Pen

You firestar. Pool of moonburst.
You turned my skin to dust. Rawblade glasstooth girl.
With your hot rage and bus ticket anywhere.
Never saw a woman run so many directions at once.
One night, you shined so bright the police came to watch.
Your bruises and shirt-shreds. How we all just stood there,
watching you shimmer. Afraid to flinch, for a faceful of claw.
You are some kind of firework. Flipswitch blues.
Broken Sundays spent towing the boulders out of you.
The Brooklyn 3am's, frenzied as an upturned autobahn.
Your porchlamp laughter. The clack and sweep and throb.
The buttered slick of you. Your sweat-bead banshee pitch.
Mother warned me. Said your sugar was a ruse. Bait.
(As if madness is calculated.) I am the cruelest kind of lover.
A coward. Afraid of the thing most dazzling.
I wished the bleak into my own blood. Prayed a flock of rotten notes.
Some afternoons, I wander through your photographs. Letters.
Wonder if the river won your war.

POEM TO TRANSLATE THE POEMS

The woman is my own regret.
The children are my friends:
they cannot reach or save me.
The birds are my eyelashes,
the wolves are my hands.
Things are making sense now.
I write my loved ones into organs
trapped inside apothecary jars.
I name the wicked beautiful
because that is what I am.
The blood is always my hunger.
My body, death. The stones
mean everything stays. Or repeats.
Raspberries and lemon rinds
tell how small and wretched I've become.
Boulders are the weight of his leaving.
The horse is a dead family member,
someone old whom I barely knew.
Blade is how he could have killed me
but instead I laughed.
Each cage is a love poem
I don't know how to deserve.
Bowls just sound good in my mouth.
The things I write to fill them
are pieces of my dying.
You is almost always me.
Thimbles safeguard my lovers
who are shrinking.
When something dies, it's my mind.
When something soars, my mind.
When something is trembling, screaming,
or trying to jump in a river,

                    my mind.

ACKNOWLEDGMENTS

Grateful acknowledgment to the editors of the following publications in which many of these poems previously appeared, sometimes in earlier versions: *Anti-; The Boiler; Cease, Cows; Danse Macabre; decomP; dirtcakes; failbetter; FRiGG; JMWW; >killauthor; The Legendary; Lunch Ticket; Monkeybicycle; Muzzle; The Nervous Breakdown; The Orange Room Review; OVS Magazine; PANK; Philadelphia Stories; Radius; Rattle; Redheaded Stepchild; Third Coast; THRUSH; Uncommon Core: Contemporary Poems for Learning and Living; Union Station Magazine; Used Furniture Review; Winter Tangerine Review;* and *Word Riot*. Further gratitude to the following organizations and individuals for recording and distribution of audio or video of select poems: *Australian Broadcasting Corporation; Indiefeed: Performance Poetry;* John Paul Davis of the *j0hnpauldavis* YouTube channel; Jeff Kay of the *speakeasynyc* YouTube channel; and *SpokenHeard: Blog Talk Radio*.

NOTES

This collection is titled with a line from the poem, "Cross the sea, Esman.," from the author's first book, *Racing Hummingbirds*.

The term "grief-induced psychosis" in this collection's description is borrowed from Todd Anderson's examination of "The Session" at *The Carletonian*.

"After the Bridal Shower" was later incorporated into a larger work titled, "Wait," coauthored with Carlos Andrés Gómez and published at *Muzzle Magazine*.

"Careful the Blood" is a Golden Shovel after "a song in the front yard" by Gwendolyn Brooks.

"Hereditary" won the Sandy Crimmins National Prize for Poetry.

"Jezebel Revisits the Book of Kings" won the Third Coast Poetry Prize.

"Brawler;" "Grief, Not Guilt;" "Poem to Translate the Poems;" and "While Writing an Ode to My Lover's Hands, He Tells Me about the Revolver" were reprinted in *Uncommon Core: Contemporary Poems for Learning and Living* by Redbeard Press.

"Daydream" reappeared at *Rookie Magazine*.

"Good Girl;" "The Sick Is an Ocean;" and "While Writing an Ode to My Lover's Hands, He Tells Me about the Revolver" were reprinted in *THRUSH Poetry Journal: an Anthology of the first two years*.

"Good Girl" reappeared at *As it Ought to Be Saturday Poetry Series*.

"How did your mother die?" reappeared as an Honorable Mention at *decomP Magazine April 2004-2014: Best of Ten Years*.

GRATITUDE

Immense gratitude to: Ian Khadan for holding me through the long, long dark and remaining. You are the most courageous person I know. My father for constant, boundless, and unflinching love. My mother for undeniable bravery. Linda Harris and Michael Carroll for taking me as your own. Brian Bean, Tamra Carlson, Laura Leach, Rhonda Harris, Beth Alvarez, Burke Harris, and Sandi Harris, for bond or blood. Eboni Hogan for every monster, for every knuckle, for the knowing. Missy Guisinger for the toughest love, for the fight and survive. My surrogate brothers: Jon Sands, Adam Falkner, Adam Bowser, Carlos Andrés Gómez, Rico Frederick, and Omar Holmon for grounding. Julie Houston and Jenn Stewart for sisterhood. Melissa Ockman for all the miles. Megan Falley for teaching me courage. Angel Nafis for truth. Rachel McKibbens for witchcraft, nurture, hammer. Duv Zaragoza and Eliel Lucero for honor. Mike Fitzgerald and Gregg Mockenhaupt for the weight. Mahogany L. Browne and Lynne Procope for the breaking. The Witches for living out loud. Phillip Gaskin. Monica Burgess. Syreeta McFadden. Connor Dooley. Catalina Ferro. Karen Grace. Jared Singer. Scott Beal. Marty McConnell. Ken Arkind. Christine Hatch. William Evans. Shira Erlichman. Joanna Hoffman. Jive Poetic. Big Mike. Elliott Smith Vacek. John Paul Davis. Victoria Lynne McCoy. Shawn Randall. David Ayllon. Corinna Bain.

Emily Kagan-Trenchard. Geoff Kagan-Trenchard. Urbana. louderARTS. Nuyorican. Taylor Mali, Jeff Kay, Wess Mongo Jolley, Justin Woo, Susan Dobbe Chase, Ryk McIntyre. Write Bloody. Stevie Edwards for the otherworld. Alex Kryger for obliging. Sarah Kay for grace, precision, spirit. Tyson Schroeder for patience. Ashley Seibels for patience. Andie Flores for patience. Derrick Brown for believing, again. Cristin O'Keefe Aptowicz for forging the path. Aulë, my prince, for mettle. And Callisto, my always girl, for teaching me kindness.

JEANANN VERLEE is a former punk rocker who collects tattoos and wears polka dots. Her first book, *Racing Hummingbirds,* earned the Independent Publisher Book Award Silver Medal for poetry. She has also been awarded the Third Coast Poetry Prize and the Sandy Crimmins National Prize for Poetry. Her work has appeared in *The New York Quarterly, Rattle, failbetter,* and *PANK,* among others, and anthologized in various publications, including *Uncommon Core: Contemporary Poems for Learning and Living, The Courage Anthology: Daring Poems for Gutsy Girls,* and *Looking for the Enemy: The Eternal Internal Gender Wars of Our Sisters Anthology.* Verlee has worked as poetry editor for *Union Station Magazine, For Some Time Now: Performance Poets of New York City,* and *Winter Tangerine Review: Fragments of Persephone,* in addition to a number of individual collections. A veteran of poetry slam, she has represented New York City ten times at the National Poetry Slam, Individual World Poetry Slam, and Women of the World Poetry Slam. For eight years, Verlee served as director of the Urbana Poetry Slam reading series, where she also acted as writing and performance coach. She has performed and facilitated workshops at schools, theatres, libraries, bookstores, dive bars, and poetry venues across North America. A proponent of human and animal rights, Verlee has also dedicated many years to activism: writing and performing theatre for social change, organizing and participating in social actions, animal rescue, and survivor advocacy. Verlee lives in New York City with her husband and their rescue pup, Aulë. She believes in you.

If You Like Jeanann Verlee, Jeanann Likes...

Heavy Lead Birdsong
Ryler Dustin

After the Witch Hunt
Megan Falley

Yarmulkes & Fitted Caps
Aaron Samuels

The New Clean
Jon Sands

Good Grief
Stevie Edwards

Write Bloody Publishing distributes and promotes great books of fiction, poetry and art every year. We are an independent press dedicated to quality literature and book design, with an office in Austin, TX.

Our employees are authors and artists so we call ourselves a family. Our design team comes from all over America: modern painters, photographers and rock album designers create book covers we're proud to be judged by.

We publish and promote 8-12 tour-savvy authors per year. We are grass-roots, D.I.Y., bootstrap believers. Pull up a good book and join the family. Support independent authors, artists and presses.

**Want to know more about Write Bloody books, authors, and events?
Join our mailing list at**

www.writebloody.com

WRITE BLOODY BOOKS

After the Witch Hunt — Megan Falley

Aim for the Head: An Anthology of Zombie Poetry — Rob Sturma, Editor

Amulet — Jason Bayani

Any Psalm You Want — Khary Jackson

Birthday Girl with Possum — Brendan Constantine

The Bones Below — Sierra DeMulder

Born in the Year of the Butterfly Knife — Derrick C. Brown

Bouquet of Red Flags — Taylor Mali

Bring Down the Chandeliers — Tara Hardy

Ceremony for the Choking Ghost — Karen Finneyfrock

Courage: Daring Poems for Gutsy Girls — Karen Finneyfrock, Mindy Nettifee & Rachel McKibbens, Editors

Dear Future Boyfriend — Cristin O'Keefe Aptowicz

Dive: The Life and Fight of Reba Tutt — Hannah Safren

Drunks and Other Poems of Recovery — Jack McCarthy

The Elephant Engine High Dive Revival anthology

Everyone I Love Is a Stranger to Someone — Annelyse Gelman

Everything Is Everything — Cristin O'Keefe Aptowicz

The Feather Room — Anis Mojgani

Gentleman Practice — Buddy Wakefield

Glitter in the Blood: A Guide to Braver Writing — Mindy Nettifee

Good Grief — Stevie Edwards

The Good Things About America — Derrick Brown & Kevin Staniec, Editors

The Heart of a Comet — Pages D. Matam

Hot Teen Slut — Cristin O'Keefe Aptowicz

I Love Science! — Shanny Jean Maney

I Love You Is Back — Derrick C. Brown

The Importance of Being Ernest — Ernest Cline

In Search of Midnight — Mike McGee

103

The Incredible Sestina Anthology — Daniel Nester, Editor

Junkyard Ghost Revival anthology

Kissing Oscar Wilde — Jade Sylvan

The Last Time as We Are — Taylor Mali

Learn Then Burn — Tim Stafford & Derrick C. Brown, Editors

Learn Then Burn 2: This Time It's Personal— Tim Stafford, Editor

Learn Then Burn Teacher's Manual — Tim Stafford & Molly Meacham, Editors

Live for a Living — Buddy Wakefield

Love in a Time of Robot Apocalypse — David Perez

The Madness Vase — Andrea Gibson

Multiverse: An Anthology of Superhero Poetry of Superhuman Proportions — Rob Sturma & Rky Mcintyre, Editors

The New Clean — Jon Sands

New Shoes on a Dead Horse — Sierra DeMulder

No Matter the Wreckage — Sarah Kay

Oh, Terrible Youth — Cristin O'Keefe Aptowicz

Our Poison Horse — Derrick C. Brown

Over the Anvil We Stretch — Anis Mojgani

Pansy— Andrea Gibson

Pole Dancing to Gospel Hymns — Andrea Gibson

Racing Hummingbirds — Jeanann Verlee

Readhead and the Slaughter King — Megan Falley

Rise of the Trust Fall — Mindy Nettifee

Scandalabra — Derrick C. Brown

Slow Dance with Sasquatch — Jeremy Radin

The Smell of Good Mud — Lauren Zuniga

Songs from Under the River — Anis Mojgani

Spiking the Sucker Punch — Robbie Q. Telfer

Strange Light — Derrick C. Brown

These Are the Breaks — Idris Goodwin

Time Bomb Snooze Alarm — Bucky Sinister

The Undisputed Greatest Writer of All Time — Beau Sia

We Will Be Shelter —Andrea Gibson, Editor

What Learning Leaves — Taylor Mali

What the Night Demands — Miles Walser

Working Class Represent — Cristin O'Keefe Aptowicz

Write About an Empty Birdcage — Elaina Ellis

Yarmulkes & Fitted Caps — Aaron Levy Samuels

The Year of No Mistakes — Cristin O'Keefe Aptowicz

Yesterday Won't Goodbye — Brian S. Ellis

CPSIA information can be obtained
at www.ICGtesting.com
Printed in the USA
FSOW02n2317070415
6218FS